Diane's Heart

Transforming Loss to Purpose and Legacy

TONYA HILL ALLEN

Copyright © 2020 by Tonya Hill Allen

All rights reserved. No part of this publication may be reproduced, distributed or transmitted in any form or by any means, including photocopying, recording, or other electronic or mechanical methods, without the prior written permission of the publisher, except in the case of brief quotations embodied in critical reviews and certain other noncommercial uses permitted by copyright law.

For permission requests, write to the author, at:
falalaenterprises@gmail.com

Diane's Heart / Tonya Hill Allen 1st. ed

ISBN Paperback: 978-1-953449-24-5
Ebook: 978-1-953449-25-2

Thank you to my beautiful mom, Diane Hill-Harrison, for leaving such a powerful legacy of love and generosity. I pray the work that we're doing in your memory and by inspiration of the Holy Spirit blesses and changes the lives of many families. Though you are not physically with me, your love lives in me and my heart is purposed to share Diane's "Heart" with the world.

To my beautiful Kings, my sons Michael-Anthony and Davis, I dedicate this book to you as record of your grandmother's love for you. Your time with her was brief on Earth, but know her love for you spans beyond a lifetime and is eternal.

CONTENTS

Foreword 7

Introduction. 9

The Story of Diane's Heart 15

Stories/Lessons from my mom 21

   The Gift Worth Sharing - Purpose 21

   The Parable of the Loaves and the Eggs - Community 25

   The Art of Sitting and Looking - Self-Care. 30

   Words Matter - Community Service 34

   Get Up From There - Spiritual/Inspirational 39

   Girlfriends - Social/Connectedness/Sisterhood. 43

   Hell, I'm Cute, Too - Mental Wellness/Mindset. 46

   There is ALWAYS Money Somewhere - Financial Management. . . 49

   Lead with Your Heart - Career Development 52

The Story That Almost Didn't Happen. 57

Diane's Heart Is My Heart 59

About the Author 61

FOREWORD

Diane was my aunt, but more of a second mom. Diane had a special heart and our entire family felt her love. I would say I was her favorite, but honestly, everyone in the family may say the same.

Diane's impact on my life is endless. My mother, her younger sister was a single mom, and Diane was always there to help us. From taking me to summer camp during my childhood years so my mom could get to work on time, to taking me shopping for college ensuring I had everything I needed and later on assisting me in career coaching which has led to a successful career and business endeavors. Diane was a special person and left a tremendous impact on me, our family, and so many more.

This book is about Diane's "Heart" and I am ecstatic that Tonya, her daughter, has decided to share her heart with the world. Tonya and I have grown to become sister and brother over the years. She's more similar to her mom than she thinks. She loves hard and at the same time is bold in her speech as she coaches you. I've watched her grow over the years to where she is no longer concerned about what people think and feel about her, but more concerned about getting it right in God's eyes and loving people as they need to be loved. I'm grateful for her and her love.

Tonya's desire to share the legacy of her mom means that thousands of single moms and their children will have a chance at a better life. As you read this book, I hope that you're able to feel Diane's Heart – her compassion, her drive, and her love, and that you're inspired to succeed and to help others.

Jermaine L. Spann

INTRODUCTION

My Story

It was spring break in 2010. My boys were 8 and 11 at the time. When asked what they wanted to do for spring break, the response wasn't to go to the beach or some grand trip or anything. It was simply to sleepover at Grandmommy's. They loved everything about her. They knew she would cook all the best homemade burgers and fries and let them order pizza and hot wings everyday if they wanted. She was their idea of FUN...and they were her EVERYTHING.

Although she had not scheduled off work that week, there was no way she would deny them spending the week with Grandmommy. While she was at work, they would spend time with her husband Michael, their new "granddaddy" whom they adored, too. In the middle of the day on Thursday, I received a call from my mom telling me she's leaving work early because she doesn't feel well and asking if I will come get the kids. I could hear the strain in her voice of not wanting them to go home early. They had made big plans for fun stuff to do over the weekend, like pancakes and Walmart toy shopping. I can count on one hand all of my mother's sick days. She never missed a beat. She was like the energizer bunny. However, the job was starting to wear on her. She was an HR director—a very demanding job—but she loved her work and the people she had worked with for so many years. It was the travel she hated. Occasional travel was fine, but this constant driving back and forth to Atlanta from Birmingham was a total buzzkill for her. She spent many evenings just "sitting and looking" trying to recover from the exhaustion of the hustle and bustle.

When I got to her house to check on her and to pick up the kids, she was in bed and her husband had taken the kids to the park so she could rest. She is red and blotchy in the face and neck area. A rash had started to develop and clearly she had a fever raging in her body.

A few weeks earlier, she had been to the doctor for a sinus infection. In early spring in Birmingham, Alabama the pollen counts from everything blooming is through the roof. In fact, she had gone back to the doctor because she was still having residual effects from the sinus infection and thought that maybe it had not cleared up.

I told her that she needed to go to the Emergency Room. The lethargy, fever and rash alarmed me a bit. She didn't feel like sitting in the ER all night, but made an appointment for the next day to see her primary care physician. Although I was worried, I didn't push since she had already made the appointment. I told her if she started to feel worse, to go to the ER immediately. She agreed just so I would leave her alone so she could get some rest.

The next day, she pushed her doctor's appointment back a few hours because she lacked the energy to even get out of the bed to get dressed. She still had a fever and was feeling horrible. Maybe it's the flu and a sinus infection? It seemed so "all of a sudden". I still thought she needed to go to the ER. Something didn't feel right to me. The rash had me concerned. I'm not a medical professional, but with children, I had come to know that a rash and fever wasn't a good combination.

She eventually muscled up the strength to get up and go to the doctor. She learned she'd caught some type of a "bug" that had been going around and the sinus infection was still lingering. She received a steroid shot and a different antibiotic and was sent home to rest and recover over the weekend.

Saturday morning, I rolled out of bed a little later than usual to make my way to the shower. I had a rough night in which I couldn't really sleep. Although my mom had gone to the doctor, subconsciously I must have still been worried that she wasn't feeling well. I tossed and turned all night and had the weirdest dream that I still remember to this day. I can't even speak of that dream.

Getting out of the shower, I heard my cell phone ring, but missed the call. I threw on my robe and ran to grab my phone. There were three missed phone calls with the last call being my grandmother, Leola. My mother's mom. I called her back. "Has anyone reached you to let you know they've taken your mom to the hospital by ambulance? Her blood pressure is low and she can't walk," she said. "Is she coherent?" I asked. "She's talking and alert, but she is still feeling awful".

They ran ALL the tests and they still could only surmise that it was some type of infection, possibly a Urinary Tract Infection (UTI). A UTI can cause all of this? Surely not. Her kidneys were not functioning properly and other organs were beginning to weaken. She needed to be transferred to the Intensive Care Unit (ICU). Lab results showed it was sepsis and now her breathing was labored, but they worked and worked and worked and finally got her breathing under control. We got to see her after waiting and praying for hours. She was smiling and looked relieved.

She said, "For a minute there, I thought y'all would be eating chicken over me this weekend."

She was referring to customs of our black community and family of the repast following a funeral where some form of chicken is usually served. We all laughed, but deep inside I was still in shock and disbelief that she came so close to death.

The plan was that her husband would stay overnight with her that night and I would stay the following night and we'd alternate as we went. I ran home to take a shower and rest up. I had been at the hospital for 14 hours. I was home for about 30 minutes, dozing off to sleep and my phone rang. It was my mother's cell number, but it was her husband's voice.

"They need to put your mom on the ventilator," he said. "Her breathing and oxygen levels are declining rapidly. She wants to talk to you."

I could barely make out what she was saying as she was gasping and struggling to breathe. I started talking and asking questions because although I knew how grave the situation was, I was in total denial that it was that bad.

"Are you praying to stay here?" I ask.

"Yes," she said.

"I'm praying for you to stay here. You can beat this, you know that, right?"

"Yes," she said. Very abruptly, she says, "I love you."

I told her, "I love you more."

She couldn't catch her breath so she passed the phone. Her breath was failing.

I made it back to the hospital, but they'd already intubated her. The doctor informed us that they have one more mega dose drug they want to try. I have since learned that this drug will either save you or kill you. It didn't work for my mom and in less than 72 hours from the time my mom left work sick, she passed. At the age of 56, one month before her 57th birthday. We later found out that her cause of death is Myocarditis. Inflammation around her heart caused by a viral infection.

Although sickness stopped her physical heart, it could not stop the legacy of her spiritual heart of love and generosity.

"Be not overcome of evil, but overcome evil with good."

ROMANS 12:21, KJV

THE STORY OF DIANE'S HEART

On March 21, 2010, my mother Diane Hill-Harrison went to be with the Lord. It was a sudden death and it sent me into a sudden shock. I can't even describe to you what it was like. She was a single mom to me, her only child and we were very close. She had me at a young age so, in a lot of ways, we grew up together. She was so much fun. From music, to fashion, decorating, cooking and all the "girly" things you can imagine, we did it. Although she was busy working and making a living for us, somehow, I never felt alone or without her. She was always there. At PTA meetings, dance performances, award programs, you name it. In our latter years, we vacationed together. We shopped together. We loved shopping together and I loved shopping with her because she would pay. We talked on the phone every day, sometimes two or three times a day. This was the norm when I was in college and even after she married just two years before her death.

She left this earth on a Sunday morning and by Tuesday I had this amazing peace overtake me. I couldn't make sense of how this could happen to someone so full of life. I can remember telling God that I didn't understand, "but I trust you God." And the only thing I was consumed with, other than making burial arrangements and the funeral service, was how I was going to honor her memory. She left this earth too soon, but I would try my best for her to never be forgotten. Because of her generous heart and her spirit to love people, I wanted to share that with the world.

At her burial service, my mother's distant cousin was standing in line to share condolences. There were so many people at her burial. It was like a receiving line at a wedding—at the cemetery of all places. One after the other, hugging me, sharing great memories and kind words, they would come. Finally, my mother's distant cousin, who was also a single mom was next. She had been in the line for a while. As we embraced, I could see the pain in her eyes and sense the warmness of her heart.

Trying to restrain the tears forming in her eyes she said, " I just felt compelled to let you know something. I was not leaving until I let you know how much your mother meant to me and why. I was about to be evicted. I couldn't pay my rent. And I had borrowed from everybody I could think of to help me. I saw your mother's face. I hadn't talked to her in a while, but I just gave her a call and asked her if she would help me. And she said, 'Absolutely, I will pay your rent.' I never imagined she would do that or that anybody would just pay my rent." What stood out to me in that conversation was when she said that my mother's actions were without judgment and condemnation and that she felt my mother was genuinely concerned. She went on to say "I have told myself that when I'm able to, I want to do the same for somebody else."

And so that was the hook. From the declaration I made on Tuesday that I would do something to honor her memory, I knew in my spirit that this was it. I would make a donation or pay someone's rent in her memory. I learned later, that wasn't even the half of it.

She was my best friend. Even though she was my mother and I didn't get it twisted, I know Mama and I know daughter, she was really my best friend. We hung out. She was a good girl, a fun girl. Her energy and smile could light up a room. I missed that fellowship. It took me about 22 months to go through the grieving process of my mother. Every day—I mean literally Every. Single. Day.—for about 22 months, I woke up crying and clutching a picture of her that I would tuck under my pillow. It was not that I didn't have peace in my spirit about where she was now. She's with the Lord. But, I missed her so much.

During this period, God started giving me very vivid dreams and visions. Dreams that I would remember when I would wake. Portions of the dreams I can remember even to this day. The vision would be that I was standing up talking to a room full of women. I would also see children in the vision. I have not spoken the full vision because it scared me as God was revealing it to me. I knew it was bigger than just me. Also during this time, I would learn of the many more stories of generosity of my mother. Stories of how she paid their utility bills, books for college, tuition, groceries, and even bail for people. Many who were either single moms or the children of single moms.

Although I was making donations and volunteering my time with different organizations, I was finally figuring out, really surrendering to the fact that it would be something greater. On an early morning before the break of day, in a state of awakening from a dream, I heard the word FOUNDATION so loud and clear. It jarred me. Fully awake now, I sat straight up in the bed.

I had never experienced anything like this. I begin to pray and seek God for revelation.

I wasn't the best student with God or maybe I wasn't the most obedient. It was kind of like the Holy Spirit was saying, "I keep coming to you because you're not getting it." Please take it from me, God won't let you miss it. He will find you. Over time and at some point in this journey, I started journaling and writing down different words that would come to me and what I could remember from the dreams. Eventually, I figured out, it wasn't one donation that I would give, it was a lifetime of donations I was being called to give.

While studying 2 Kings 4:1-7, the words seemed to leap off the page.

> *4 Now there cried a certain woman of the wives of the sons of the prophets unto Elisha, saying, Thy servant my husband is dead; and thou knowest that thy servant did fear the Lord: and the creditor is come to take unto him my two sons to be bondmen.*
>
> *² And Elisha said unto her, What shall I do for thee? Tell me, what hast thou in the house? And she said, Thine handmaid hath not any thing in the house, save a pot of oil.*
>
> *³ Then he said, Go, borrow thee vessels abroad of all thy neighbours, even empty vessels; borrow not a few.*
>
> *⁴ And when thou art come in, thou shalt shut the door upon thee and upon thy sons, and shalt pour out into all those vessels, and thou shalt set aside that which is full.*
>
> *⁵ So she went from him, and shut the door upon her and upon her sons, who brought the vessels to her; and she poured out.*
>
> *⁶ And it came to pass, when the vessels were full, that she said unto her son, Bring me yet a vessel. And he said unto her, There*

is not a vessel more. And the oil stayed.

7 Then she came and told the man of God. And he said, Go, sell the oil, and pay thy debt, and live thou and thy children of the rest.

In that passage of scripture, the woman in this story is a single mother. The prophet asked her, "What do you have in your house?" Her first answer was, "Nothing." This was also my answer to God as I was getting clearer about this assignment. Then the woman remembered, except a pot oil. I had this revelation in that moment that I am supposed to share my gift, the legacy of my mother, to start a nonprofit serving single mothers and their children. This was my "pot of oil." The first act of faith that I would be challenged with was to TELL MANY, NOT A FEW.

The first opportunity to share this vision came sooner than I expected the very next day. I was volunteering in the Children's ministry at church. One of the parents recognized me as Diane's daughter.

She said so warmly, "You're Diane's daughter aren't you?"

I didn't recognize the person and had never met her. That didn't surprise me, my mother knew a lot of people.

After confirming that, indeed, I was Diane's daughter, she went on to say, "I think about her all the time. How are you doing?"

Now, I sensed that I was supposed to tell her about this vision I had and so I was nervous as I could be—fearful that I would look and sound foolish about all this "God stuff." I opened my mouth and began to tell her that I was planning to start a foundation in my mother's honor and it would serve single mothers and their children. She thought it was an awesome idea and reached into her purse to find her checkbook to MAKE A DONATION.

At this point, I only had this revelation from God. There wasn't even a name for the organization let alone a checking account to receive a donation. This was confirmation that I was on the right track. In 2016, I started Diane's Heart, a nonprofit in the memory of my mother Diane Hill-Harrison, to provide a support system for single moms and their children. I am on a mission to share with you and the world, Diane's Heart.

This book is a collection of memories and life lessons that bear witness to the heart and spirit of my mother. Each story reflects the pillars of the nonprofit and our mission to teach, give to and serve single mothers, their children and our community. Some of the stories and the names of people have been slightly changed to distort the identities of people.

Beauty for Ashes, Joy for Mourning and Praise for Heaviness.
ISAIAH 61:3

To console those who mourn in Zion,
To give them beauty for ashes, The oil of joy for mourning,
The garment of praise for the spirit of heaviness;
That they may be called trees of righteousness,
The planting of the LORD, that He may be glorified."

STORIES/LESSONS FROM MY MOM

THE GIFT WORTH SHARING
PURPOSE

It was early on a Saturday morning. I could smell the aroma of Ajax, Lemon Pledge, and lemon scented ammonia before I opened my eyes. Aretha Franklin was blaring through the WHOLE house and so was my mom as she was singing, cleaning, and dancing to EVERY tune. When I was younger and we lived with my grandparents, I would be up watching cartoons and eating breakfast while these shenanigans were on display. Now that I was in Middle school and she had her own apartment, cleaning the bathroom, my bedroom and ALL the vacuuming of EVERY carpet were now my chores. I begged her the night before to please let me sleep late Saturday morning. For her that meant until 8am. She'd already been up since 6am cleaning and fellowshipping with the girls—Aretha Franklin, Gladys Knight, Diana Ross and Patti LaBelle. She obliges to let me sleep in—or so I think.

The night before, I fell asleep in the den doing what I loved most: writing and dreaming of all the wonderful things in life I could do or become. She had instilled that in me all of my life—to dream of what could be. Nothing was impossible. Writing in my notebook or diary was my escape to dream. Reading was her escape from reality. The reality of being a single mom with no help from my father who lived just across town. Going it alone with the support of her parents while also being support to her siblings. She was the eldest child of seven and EVERYBODY looked up to her. She had made it..."kinda."

My 7th grade Homeroom teacher Mrs. Gibson, who was also my

English teacher, had given me an assignment. The assignment was to write about how I could change the world. She was my first ever White teacher. For that matter, this was the first time I'd attended school with kids of other races. I thought she was the Queen of England. I was fascinated and a little terrified by how she commanded respect in her classroom. She would have these individual lessons with each student and she made the mistake of telling me I had excellent writing skills. Talk about head-swell. I would write on napkins if I could. I would diagram everybody's sentences in my head as they spoke to grade if it was "proper" grammar. It was years later when I found out she told everybody they had excellent writing skills. I just happened to be one who believed her. Hence, the reason on a Friday night I'm writing about changing the world.

A late night commercial featuring children with enlarged stomachs and flies on their faces is what I woke up to at 1am. I had fallen asleep on the sofa with my notebook and pen still in my hands. I was moved, touched, and heart-broken as I watched and heard a woman plead for me to send money to starving children in Africa.

How could we live so well in America with all the food we could imagine? Not just any food. My mama's food. She could cook like nobody's business. Especially her homemade Macaroni and Cheese.

So, I start back writing. How can I change the world? Voila! That's it. I can raise money to send to the children in Africa. I can also help Emma, the girl I sat beside in fourth grade. She was so poor and everyone in our class knew it. I could feel her shame and always wondered if she was okay. I could start a food bank and ask people to donate food and we could send boxes of food to these hungry children. Before I knew it, it was 3am and there were three pages of things I could do to change the world. Let me get to bed. Those chores will be waiting on me soon enough.

I heard her footsteps headed to my room. Is it already 8 o'clock?!?!

She calls my name, but it's a very soft, muffled tone. Not the usual smiling and laughing playful tone as she opens the curtains to let God's "good sunshine" in as she yells from the top of her lungs: "get up sunshine...it's time to rise and shine". This morning is different. She's holding my notebook that I left on the den table. I knew she read my stuff, diaries and all. There was nothing coming through the threshold of any door in her house that was "private." I stopped pretending that I was still asleep and rolled over to see what was going on. She was standing there in tears and all choked up. I sat straight up.

"Are you okay?" I asked.

She had these uncontrollable tears streaming down her face, and I heard her say, "I'm so proud of you. I'm so proud that you know what it means to share."

LESSON

Sharing. It sounds so basic but that was the foundation of how she saw everything. Who she was, whatever she had and whatever she was doing. She had learned a secret. It's better, more fun, and more fulfilling if you share it. I had watched my mom all of my life help others and share her time, money, and love with so many. She did it effortlessly and with passion.

Definition of Share

Share
/SHer/
Verb. give a portion of (something) to another or others.

HOW IT INFUSES THE WORK WE DO TODAY

Like the single mom in the scripture in 2 Kings 4:1-7, we recognize that in pouring out what we have, God in turn fills us with joy and wholeness. It is in this inspiration that we serve the women and children of Diane's Heart. As we share our gifts of love and generosity, others are filled and we are replenished.

THINGS YOU CAN DO RIGHT NOW TO MAKE A DIFFERENCE BY SHARING

- ♥ Make a donation. There is so much need. A donation in any amount goes a long way to help charities serve the populations depending on their programs.

- ♥ Open your heart. Don't judge how someone got to where they are. It could have been you if not but for the grace of God.

- ♥ Listen. Be that listening ear to someone who needs to make a tough decision. Sometimes they don't need advice, but rather someone to hear them out so they can get clear in their own thoughts.

- ♥ Provide access. If you're on a board, or a member of a professional organization, and recognize there is no diversity, change that. Recommend and actively seek to include people of different races, gender, religion, and ethnicity to participate.

- ♥ Volunteer your time. For many small nonprofits, your time is just as valuable as your money. Offer your help to perform office or clerical work, manual labor for setup or clean-up at events, making deliveries, etc. There is ALWAYS a role to fulfill.

THE PARABLE OF THE LOAVES AND THE EGGS
COMMUNITY

Our next-door neighbor Mrs. Ernestine was a hot mess. One thing about her though, she didn't take any mess. My mom, who was a single parent, was at work when I got home from school. I was a latch-key kid. Mrs. Ernestine would keep an eye out for me. When I say she didn't miss anything, I mean SHE DIDN'T MISS ANYTHING. She knew everything that happened on the WHOLE block. And if it wasn't right or clean, she was gonna tell it. I couldn't open the door or let anyone in if my mother was not home. There was no need for a pass code because I could not open the door for anyone, not even Jesus. Well, except Mrs. Ernestine.

Mrs. Ernestine's daughter fell on some hard times. I never heard the full discussion, but let's just say she was away for a while. She sent her kids down south to Alabama to live with Mrs. Ernestine. The boy was around 3 years old and the girl was 6 or 7 years old. The kids had come to visit often during the summer and holidays. So, we knew them well.

At some point, Mrs. Ernestine fell on hard times, too. She was knocking on the door to borrow a "few" eggs and a "few" slices of bread just about every other day. I couldn't pretend that no one was home because as I said, she didn't miss ANYTHING. Also, I had to always keep the screen door locked. A dead giveaway that someone is home. This was now becoming a habit. It was happening every other day of this particular week until I felt the need to mention it to my mother. She had pretty much borrowed the whole loaf of bread and a dozen eggs.

I tell my mom that I think Mrs. Ernestine is taking advantage of us. After all, I'm now in high school and I know what it means and looks like to be taken advantage of. Mrs. Ernestine has a husband, too, as I pointed out to my mom that she didn't have one to help her. You would have thought I had just called her a liar to her face. (ALL black kids know you 'gone' die if you call your mom a liar). Although we were very close and sometimes seemed more like friends and sisters than mother and daughter, the one thing you were not going to do was be disrespectful. She made sure I didn't get it twisted and that I always knew who was the mom and who was the child. Oh, she could put you in your place.

"Who died and made you Queen?" she asked me. What has it cost you to give her bread and eggs? When did you get a job to pay for groceries?"

I knew I was about to get a sermon. My mother loved a good debate and she wanted to hear my thoughts. I think she wanted to hear my thoughts to make sure my heart was in the right place and so she could check me and get me back in line when I was not acting like the child she raised.

"Have you noticed when Mrs. Ernestine borrows a lot? Take a look at the calendar and tell me today's date." It was near the end of the month.

She then said, "When people are on fixed incomes or certain pay schedules, the money may run out before the next pay cycle. In this case, before the first of the month."

Then she said, "Open the freezer and look at all the food you have. What if it was empty, would you want someone to let you borrow bread and eggs?"

I don't know if I was being smart or dumb, but I always had a response.

"Well, I say, it's one thing to borrow, but it's another thing to pay back. When she goes to the grocery store, I don't see her knocking on the door to give us eggs and bread."

Boom, I thought I had her.

So my mother asked, "How many times did you come home from school by yourself and Mrs. Ernestine didn't check on you?"

"Never," I replied.

She always checked on me and if I was late, she would be sitting on the front porch asking what took me so long. She was so nosey, I thought. "How many times did you feel scared or afraid to be home by yourself?" A few times but I would call Mrs. Ernestine or go sit on the porch with her until you got home.

"Have you ever seen me pay her for any of that?" she asked.

I said, "No."

Her response was, "Consider the bread and eggs my payment to her. She doesn't owe me anything and I owe her every slice and every egg she needs. She was how I could keep a job and stay sane not worrying about you. She kept you out of trouble. She did that out of love for us."

"Has Mrs. Ernestine always borrowed eggs and bread from us?"

"No," I said.

"Do you really think she would ask if she didn't need them? Do you think she's just borrowing eggs and bread because she can? Don't answer—listen. The goal is to one day be able to buy her groceries before she has to ask. But for right now, we'll just share what we have."

LESSON

When I was younger, I thought my mother was weak for how she gave to a fault to people who sometimes never paid her back or were able to ever help her out financially. As I've matured, I've come to realize that giving was really her strength. Moreover, being able to give without expectation of return was her sweet spot. She recognized the blessing was in the giving and that God was the ultimate provider.

It takes a village to raise a child. She cared for Mrs. Ernestine's grandchildren like they were her own. Until we as a community or nation have that kind of concern and commitment to our neighbors and fellow citizens, we will never realize how truly powerful we can be.

HOW IT INFUSES THE WORK WE DO TODAY

It is with this love that we create a community—a safe place for our moms to discuss, share, connect, and embrace each other.

THINGS YOU CAN DO RIGHT NOW TO MAKE A DIFFERENCE BY CREATING COMMUNITY

- 💜 While buying groceries, buy extra groceries that include meat, veggies, and dessert (a full meal) and give to someone you know has fallen on hard times or could use a break. Give to a college student, a single mom, or a homeless shelter.

- 💜 Buy one-month supply of diapers, wipes, and milk for a single mom even if you think she's doing well financially. She could still use the help.

- Put together a gift basket with snacks, hand lotion, and beauty hacks and give to a single mom and let her know that she's doing a great job with her kids.

- Create a monthly neighborhood wellness check-in. Especially for the elderly or people who live alone. Sometimes just letting people know you care can be the difference in life or death.

- Buy wi-fi hotspots and donate to families with children who do not have in-home wifi. This will help with virtual learning and access to learning resources, books, and videos.

THE ART OF SITTING AND LOOKING
SELF-CARE

I was a very talkative child, at least to my mom. She always seemed to want to hear what I had to say. She never rushed me and always made me feel like what I was saying to her was the best thing she had ever heard. I was ALWAYS the center of her attention. That attention only made me want to talk more.

As soon as Christmas catalogs from Sears and JCPenny came in the mail and all of the commercials featuring new toys just in time for Christmas started airing on television, I started telling my mom what I wanted. This was an everyday thing, let her tell you. This is when I first started making lists. As soon as I could write and somewhat spell, she taught me how to make a list. This was so she could buy some time to hear herself think and get a little peace and quiet. She would often refer to this as her time for "sitting and looking" while I was busy with making my list. To this day, lists are a fundamental way of being for me. I used a list of ideas to start the nonprofit, I make lists every day in my business. I'm even using a list now to write this book.

I became conditioned to believe that "sitting and looking" was a thing, just for the two of us. That meant, the phone could ring, but we were not going to answer it because we were "sitting and looking." It also meant that cooking was not even an option because she was not "looking" in the direction of the stove. It was sandwich or cereal night. Even though it was only 6pm: "Go ahead and take your bath and get your pajamas on because we weren't leaving the house for ANYTHING OR ANYONE." As much as she loved reading romance novels, that book wouldn't be touched when we're sitting and looking. We were not "doing," we were "being." The ONLY thing I could do was write my lists and as I got older, write in my diary or notebook.

You may ask "sitting and looking" at what? Sometimes it would be nothing, not even the television. On occasion, the radio would be playing in the background. But honestly, she would be looking with a low gaze and sometimes just staring blankly at the wall. Eventually, it would yield to a peaceful, well-needed nap.

There was a particularly hectic time in life for my mom. She was laid off from her job as an internal auditor for an insurance company where she worked for almost 10 years. She had helped other people get jobs there which made it particularly hard for her because they weren't being laid off. The work she was doing was being relocated to the corporate office out of state while some of the other functions remained local. I can remember how worried sick she was wondering how she would be able to survive without a job. Fortunately, her manager at the insurance company made a few calls and recommended her to a friend who had an opening where he worked. She did not even miss one day of work. She was laid off on a Friday and started her new job with the new company on the following Monday. That didn't stop her from NEVER wanting to be in the situation ever again. She had learned a lesson about not being financially prepared for disaster. Never again.

She took a part-time job to pay off credit card debt and build up her savings. The work was easy. It was similar to the audit work she previously did for the insurance company. What was not easy was adding an additional 20 hours a week on to a 40 hour work week learning a new job while juggling raising a pre-teen by herself, PTA meetings at the school, cooking, cleaning, buying groceries, paying bills, and trying to have some semblance of a social life. Let's just say we had a lot of "sitting and looking" during this time. She was exhausted.

My mother was very outgoing and was always on-the-go. She attended everybodys' birthday party, wedding, baby shower, funeral, etc. She did not miss a gathering. She was quite the socialite. In addition, she was often the organizer for the events for our extended family as well. She planned family reunions, family dinners, and family vacations. Thanksgiving and Christmas were especially grand as she celebrated them BIG-BIG with all of her home-cooked food that she spent hours preparing. Let's not forget all of the fabulous gifts she loved shopping and wrapping, but most of all giving.

As much as she loved all of this, when it was time to sit and look, she was sitting and looking. Period.

A few weeks before she died, I could tell in her voice she was tired. She had been on one of those work trips to Atlanta and back. The drain of the pesky lingering sinus infection was only making things worse. She had called to check in to let me know she was home from her work trip. Making small talk she asked what I was doing. I rattled my list of things I needed to do. When I asked her what she was doing, we said in unison, "SITTING AND LOOKING."

LESSON

I came to know and use "sitting and looking" as a form of self-care when I became a mother. I had no idea of even the concept when my mother was doing this. I really thought sitting and looking was a thing people do. Only to realize many years later it was a form of self-preservation and mental/emotional recovery. My mother was unapologetic about that time and I have learned to be likewise. It is vitally important to take time for yourself so that you function from your overflow, not emptiness.

HOW IT INFUSES THE WORK WE DO TODAY

At Diane's Heart, we pamper our moms. While financial resources are important, we know that emotional resources are just as critical. We make sure gift items that we provide are especially "girly" and are special treats for her as a woman and as a mom. We provide child-care at no cost at all of our in-person events. We believe it is essential for our moms to have time to relax and rejuvenate without worrying about the care and concern of their kids. We understand that sometimes you just need a minute to gather yourself. We operate by the instructions of the flight attendants: "Put your oxygen mask on first before assisting others."

"You cannot pour from an empty vessel". You at least need a little oil. 2 Kings 4:1-7 (Tonya's interpretation).

THINGS YOU CAN DO RIGHT NOW TO MAKE A DIFFERENCE BY SUPPORTING SELF-CARE

- 💜 Offer free baby-sitting for a single mom. This can really make a difference for grocery shopping, hair appointments, or just a mental break to get a nap.

- 💜 Give a gift basket full of bath bombs, lotions, essential oils, candles, and other pampering and relaxation gift items to a deserving, hardworking, and probably tired single mom.

- 💜 Pay for a housekeeper to clean the home of a single mom.

- 💜 Donate a portion of your paid time off to a single mom at work. There is never enough time to get everything done or be present for the dance recital. Heaven forbid someone gets sick.

- 💜 Give gift cards for a special treat like coffee, doughnuts, manicure, pedicure, or massage.

WORDS MATTER
COMMUNITY SERVICE

My mother would do anything to promote and maintain my positive self-esteem. NOTHING was too good for Diane's daughter. She worked hard to make sure that I had the right perspective on who I am in this big world. For her, what you said mattered. She didn't play about people "calling me out of my name." For that matter, she abhorred nicknames. When I shortened my name to Tonya in college to navigate prejudice and racism at the recommendation of a college professor, she put up her own resistance and called me LaTonya just to make her point.

When I was in high school, there was a meeting at the school. I don't remember what was discussed because I wasn't really paying close attention. I was only there because my mom was coming straight from work to get to the meeting on time. She didn't have time to take me to my grandmother's. All I remember was the ride home and what felt like a lesson that I had to learn right then. She began her dissertation with, "Don't ever let anyone label you."

She went on, "You are not disadvantaged, they are greedy. You are not underprivileged, your privileges were stolen and denied to you. The only thing you're 'at-risk' for is being great."

She then told me about why we even had the Civil Rights Movement. Now, all of this I've heard numerous times before because we live in Birmingham, Alabama. The horror stories she would tell about having dental work performed without anesthetic to block the pain because it was not administered to black kids. That was considered a privilege back then.

I knew her soapbox was out and she was on it when she started to talk about "over the mountain." In Birmingham, AL, the city and the suburban areas are separated by Red Mountain. The higher income white people were known to live "over the mountain." My mother harped on that because she was very familiar with unfair housing practices and the redlining of neighborhoods. Her point was always that either side is "over the mountain" depending on from which side of the mountain you start.

I didn't realize that we were "low income" until I got to high school. I went to a high school with kids from all of over the city of Birmingham. There was an entrance exam required to be accepted to attend Ramsay Alternative High School. It was rumored to be the school where all the "smart kids" went to school. On top of that, it was a public school that was touted to provide a private school, college preparatory learning experience. My mother believed in education and she was not going to stop until I was accepted at this school.

The experience was quite that of a culture shock. It was on the south side of Birmingham, about 30 minutes from where we lived. I had to ride the school bus to get there. An event all to itself. Then there were the obviously wealthy kids and the other kids who perpetrated like they were wealthy. It was a melting pot of different races, socio economic levels, and backgrounds. This school had so much to offer academically. I had a hard time choosing an elective. I was fascinated by fashion and design and knew that someday we would go to Paris. My mother encouraged me to take French as a foreign language elective. I did and I LOVED it. This was during the time of the night-time soap opera, Dynasty. I fell in love with the character Dominique Devereaux played by the incomparable Diahann Carroll. My mom and I would watch just to see the outfits she would wear. What glamour! Dominique became my French alias during class that year.

I wasn't aware there was this big trip to Paris that was offered at the school. It was thousands of dollars. I can remember bringing the flyer home to my mom wanting so badly to go. She was not going to even get my hopes up. She said, the cost of this trip is about the amount of money I have saved so far for your college tuition. You won't be able to go on this trip. I said something so smart-aleck teenager like, "Oh, I forgot we're 'low income'." That sent her into a frenzy. That her child is now using a label she fought so hard not to be defined by.

Her response, "You may not be able to go to Paris right now, but you WILL LEARN AND KNOW EVERYTHING there is to learn and know about Paris."

So during the time the students who could afford to go on the Paris trip were in Paris, I was going to the library to check out every book I could find about Paris museums, architecture, wars, cuisine, fashion, lifestyle....all of it. This was of course before the world wide web as we know it now. It was called an Encyclopedia back then. We went to the Birmingham Museum of Art to visit exhibitions to learn about All THINGS FRENCH to ad nauseum.

When I finally traveled to Paris in 2019 on a girlfriends trip to celebrate a friend's milestone birthday, I was overcome with emotion and memories of my mom and how she wanted me to get to Paris. I had always hoped it would be the two of us on one of our mother-daughter vacations. Standing in front of the Eiffel Tower was a surreal moment. It was satisfying to see the buildings and museums and remember them from ALL of the books she made me read some 30 years ago. There were moments of sadness of missing her but there were also moments of silly giggles as I reflected on how my smart mouth bought me a French lesson I will never forget.

LESSON

The words "Low Income" are not about your intelligence. The words "Under Privileged" are not about your value and the word "disadvantaged" is not about your worth. Being born makes you matter. Words do not define you. What you believe about yourself is what defines you.

HOW IT INFUSES THE WORK WE DO TODAY

My mother was a lifelong resident of the Ensley community in Birmingham. She believed: if they don't want me in their neighborhoods, I will build mine up. To this day, I still own her residence as rental property and to keep resources in Ensley. Through the nonprofit, Diane's Heart, we've hosted all of our in person events in the Ensley Entertainment District to target and reach single moms in the Ensley neighborhood and to invest our dollars in the community she loved so dearly.

THINGS YOU CAN DO RIGHT NOW TO MAKE A DIFFERENCE THROUGH COMMUNITY SERVICE

- ♥ Register to vote and exercise your right to vote for local, state, and national elections.

- ♥ Run for office. Representation matters. Your side of the story adds a different perspective and can shift outcomes, decisions, and resources.

- ♥ Be sensitive about the words you use around children. We can only rise to or above the level of our thinking. If we're going to use labels, let's make sure they are positive labels.

- 💜 Host a block party and provide food and entertainment for the kids in your hood. It's a small price to pay to keep children engaged.

- 💜 Offer to repair or pay for repairs for the home of a single mom for painting, yard work, or general maintenance.

GET UP FROM THERE
SPIRITUAL/INSPIRATIONAL

I watched my mom face many challenges over the years, but she didn't stay there for long. I knew when she would hit a "speed bump" because her playful almost child-like wonder and curiosity would become solemn and quiet. She didn't let me know everything that she would face, but she definitely didn't hide it if I asked or questioned her. What I knew is that whatever she faced, she wasn't going to stay there for long. She didn't have time for self-pity or time to slow down. She had too much life to live. It was like, "Cry and move on, honey. Ain't nobody got time for that."

No such time was it more evident than when I was facing my own bump. I had just delivered my first child. Mind you, she was more excited about this baby than EVERYBODY. She made it to the hospital before we did (even though I told her I thought I was having Braxton Hicks contractions and not the real ones). She was there for the ENTIRE labor, delivery, and recovery. We were in this new, state of the art birthing suite where the room transformed to accommodate labor, delivery, and recovery. So, we never left the room. She thought that was the coolest thing, but kept asking when they were going to take the baby to the nursery. As the excitement calmed down and I made my mom finally put the baby in the crib, I started drifting off to sleep. I was exhausted. At some point, I woke up and she's standing over the baby in the crib just watching him. She tells me to press the button to call the nurse to check on the baby. She noticed the baby was breathing fast and something just didn't seem right to her. I immediately pressed the button and told the nurse and in 0.2 seconds 2 nurses and a doctor showed up in the room. The baby had swallowed meconium during delivery. His lungs are wet and he will need to go to the Neonatal Intensive Care Unit (NICU). This wasn't quite the nursery my mom had been asking about.

It was time for me to be released from the hospital. It just happens to be my birthday. My mother is sitting with me when the doctor comes in. I'm able to be released, but the baby will have to stay longer. The doctor couldn't tell me exactly how much longer. I freak completely out. I told my mom and the doctor, "I can't leave my baby here."

She looks at me realizing that I'm about to completely meltdown and come apart. She steps out of the room with the doctor. She has made arrangements for me to stay in the hospital room for two additional days. This is her "birthday treat" for me. She's paying for my extended stay.

After the two days, the baby is still not able to be released to go home. My mother enters the room. She doesn't even say hello. She walks right over to the window and pulls open the curtains to let God's "good" sunshine in as she yells from the top of her lungs, "Get up sunshine… it's time to rise and shine."

"Did they release the baby or something? What is going on?" I asked.

"No, they have not released the baby, but this is not the Hyatt Hotel, this is a hospital. There is nothing wrong with you. You got to get up from there! You can't stay here. Where your mind goes, your whole life goes. Get your mind right. The doctors are taking excellent care of the baby. It's time for you to go home."

In an instant, it was like I snapped out of a fog. The heaviness rolled away and God's "good sunshine" seemed to flood my heart. She helped me get dressed like she did when I was a little girl. She put bright red lipstick on me. In her mind, a good red lipstick could wake up your whole face.

Fast forward to weeks after her death, I'm laying in my bed at home. I could not get up the energy to return to normal. I called in and requested an additional week off of work. The calls and visits had slowed down drastically. It was almost like the world had moved on, but I was still standing still, just stuck. But one person called me everyday to check on me. Of all people, it was my grandmother, Leola, my mom's mom. We called her mama. Surely, she was grieving herself. They were best friends, too. They were as close as she and I were to each other. On this particular day, I was struggling. I was at peace that she was in Heaven, but I just missed her presence so much. I missed her voice and her laughter. I missed the smell of her perfume and her red lipstick. I missed everything about her.

It's about 2pm. She starts in with her questioning. Leola could ask questions like Oprah Winfrey and have you telling her all of your deepest secrets in 10 minutes flat.

"This is the third day in a row that I've called you and you've been in that bed," she said. "You got to get up from there! You can't stay here. Where your mind goes, your whole life goes. Get your mind right. God's got your mama. She lived a good life. Now you have to live yours."

It was like my mom was speaking to me through my grandmother. The same exact words that I'd heard before. The same exact energy that I had witnessed of her when she hit bumps. There was no time to waste just lingering in the sadness and darkness of it all.

After we hung up and she made me promise her I was getting up, I finally got out of the bed. I walked over to the window and opened the curtain to let God's "good sunshine" in and said to myself, "Get up sunshine...it's time to rise and shine."

LESSON

In life, we will all face challenges or "bumps" as my mom and grandmother would call them. It's important that we process the challenge and go through to get to the other side. It becomes a problem when we wallow in it and become stuck.

HOW IT INFUSES THE WORK WE DO TODAY

All of our events and programs have an inspirational and spiritual component. We provide life coaching, mentoring, and training on how to move forward in life.

THINGS YOU CAN DO RIGHT NOW TO MAKE A DIFFERENCE THROUGH INSPIRATION

- 💜 Donate a free coaching or counseling session if you're a practicing Life Coach or Licensed Counselor.

- 💜 Invite a single mom to join your life group or small group.

- 💜 Provide free or discounted legal services.

- 💜 Cover a single mom and her children in prayer.

- 💜 Start a program in your community that creates a support system for single moms.

GIRLFRIENDS
SOCIAL/CONNECTEDNESS/SISTERHOOD

My mom was the eldest of seven children, four girls and three boys. She was close to all of her siblings but the girls shared a special "girl squad" bond. Wherever you saw Diane, you saw Leola (my grandmother's namesake), Gloria or Cynthia. As far back as I can remember, my mother also had a sister circle of girlfriends that she hung out or visited with on a regular basis. They stayed in contact and would be there to help in a moment's notice whether it was happy times, sad times, or in-between times. I remember The Foxy 8 Social and Savings Club of the 70s and 80s. They wore matching shirts and I thought they were so cool. I couldn't wait to grow up and be just like them. They always seemed to have fun and really enjoy good conversations and would make the best food. They were more social than savings, I think. Although, this was how they made and saved money for Christmas toys and gifts. They would have the best Fish Fries and Barbeque plate sales on the weekend. I so looked forward to playing with the children of the other moms in the S&S club. I truly believe these were early lessons in how to run a business and offer excellent customer service. It was like a well-oiled machine and each girlfriend played her part. After everyone could have access to personal checking and savings accounts and had new and better jobs, the need for the S&S club fell away. Now they were purely social to be social.

My mom had different sets of girlfriends. There were her work friends, her neighbor friends, her cousin friends, and so on. You get it, she always surrounded herself with girlfriends. There was power in embracing other women in their journey. There was a connectedness in the community and fellowship of other women. At the base of this was her powerful gift of being inclusive. In a world that wanted to make people feel disadvantaged, at-risk, less than, etc., there was this hope of friendship that said we're all the same. We may be in different phases of the journey, but we are all on the same journey. Some were single moms like her, some were married, some divorced, and some didn't have children but they all loved having a good time whenever they were together.

When she started her new position in Human Resources, she was hoping to find a career. Her journey would lead to a successful career culminating in her becoming a Director of Human Resources. However, more than a career, she found another community of women where she felt connection. She would always express how this team felt like family to her. Several of them over the years would become like aunties to me. One in particular who hosted my first baby tea, cooked me pot roast and peas after my mother's death, and would eventually Chair the nonprofit bearing my mother's memory. Another who calls to check on me regularly (still) and supports the nonprofit financially and with legal opinion.

It was my circle of girlfriends, The Vivas, who rallied around me in support with financial donations and volunteering at events to help get the nonprofit off of the ground. Similar to my mom's social and savings club, Viva started out with a mission as a book club. However, some of us were there only for the social part of the gathering. Now we're purely social, too. The sister circle continues.

LESSON

There is nothing like good girlfriends. Period.

HOW IT INFUSES THE WORK WE DO TODAY

Our desire is that no mom ever feels alone on this journey. This is a safe place to get guidance, make friends, stay encouraged and motivated. Most of all, it's a place to make your dreams a reality.

THINGS YOU CAN DO RIGHT NOW TO MAKE A DIFFERENCE BY CREATING CONNECTEDNESS

- 💜 Donate to Diane's Heart or a nonprofit that supports and builds connection and community for single moms and/or children.

- 💜 Start a prayer circle, bible study or special interest group and invite people to participate and to bring a friend. The invitation alone could change a life.

- 💜 Rave about, recommend or share information in your Social Media feed about nonprofit programs available in your community. Sometimes the resources are available but the people who need them may not know about them.

- 💜 Smile an authentic smile when interacting. It welcomes people to open up to get to know you.

- 💜 Ask how you can help. Most people won't ask for help but will not turn down the offer for help.

HELL, I'M CUTE, TOO
MENTAL WELLNESS/MINDSET

I'm lounging on the sofa in the den watching the television while my mom is cooking in the kitchen which is a few feet away in a combined area. I'm not really listening to what she's saying, but as soon as I hear her voice get louder as she proclaims, "Hell, I'm cute, too." One hand on her hip, the other stirring the food while the phone is nestled between her shoulder and ear, I took note. Now I'm starting to eavesdrop to hear all of the "juice" going on in this conversation. From what I could tell, one of her girlfriends is in her insecure feelings about how her ex-husband's new wife is so pretty. My mom went on to say something along the lines of "God didn't stop passing out pretty when Ruthie (the new wife) came along."

Although now I'm a certified life coach, I must say my mother was doing this back when it wasn't even a profession and she wasn't getting paid a dime to do it. The way she framed things could penetrate your thinking and transform your mind. This was one of those times when something she said stuck with me and helped me get through my awkward teenage years. I was very slim, tall with very chiseled features. It was uncommon in my black community to be so thin. Most women, even teenage girls were voluptuous and well endowed. Not to mention, I had an aunt who once told me I was an ugly little baby. The combination of not being considered pretty and having body image issues was beginning to form a negative self-image in me.

As usual, when she got off the phone and there was something she thought I needed to know or learn, she started teaching—whether I wanted to hear it or not. It was almost like she had a 6th sense that this was an issue I was dealing with.

She started out telling me, "If you don't think you're cute, pretty, fabulous, (you fill in the blank), then nobody else will. This is the only face and body God gave you. If he thought it was good enough, then it is good enough."

Years later, this topic would resurface. She had a friend who was stunningly beautiful and equally secure in herself. My mother wraps up a phone call with this friend. As usual, she had something to teach me about the conversation they just had. This friend, she believes, is misunderstood and gets a hard time from other women because she is so pretty and she is so confident. I think people are intimidated by her which prevents them from getting to know her. When you get to know her, people discover that she has a beautiful heart and her feelings are easily hurt. She will do anything to help if you're in need. So I asked why she wasn't intimidated by her? Her response, "Hell, I'm cute, too!"

LESSON

How you interact, engage and view others depends on the filters you're looking through and your own self confidence. How you experience someone can intimidate or motivate you depending on how you see yourself. How you see yourself colors how you view others.

My mother believed in "getting your mind right." So, whether that means getting a coach or therapy, changing your environment or setting boundaries, do what you have to in order to preserve your mental wellness and mindset.

HOW IT INFUSES THE WORK WE DO TODAY

Our Adopt A Mom™ Coaching program focuses on setting and achieving one BIG goal and identifying and eliminating limiting beliefs and mindset blocks that hinder us from reaching our goal. We focus on building confidence and maintaining a positive mindset as the "force" to push beyond fear to tap into purpose and fulfillment.

THINGS YOU CAN DO RIGHT NOW TO MAKE A DIFFERENCE BY PROMOTING MENTAL WELLNESS AND POSITIVE MINDSET

- ❤ Give. Helping someone else takes the focus off of your problems or needs.

- ❤ Show gratitude to people who have helped you in some way by sending notes or cards to simply say "Thank You".

- ❤ Exercise for at least 30 minutes most days of the week. Even if it's walking around your house or dancing to Beyonce' while you cook.

- ❤ Help children, especially tweens and teens, focus on and stand strong in their beliefs instead of their looks. Mentoring matters.

- ❤ Get help. Even with good self-care practices, help from a professional doctor or therapist may be the "ultimate" self-care tool.

THERE IS ALWAYS MONEY SOMEWHERE
FINANCIAL MANAGEMENT

There is a knock at the door and I notice it's someone that I don't recognize. I wait for my mom to open the door. She immediately recognizes the young man and opens the door. He passes her an envelope through the door never entering the house and says, "My mom told me to bring this to you." She opens the envelope and gives him a single bill from the money that's inside. From where I'm sitting, I could see that it was a twenty dollar bill. She has a brief small talk with him and he leaves.

This all happened in less than 2 minutes. This is really peculiar, I thought, because she doesn't turn to tell me anything about what just transpired or teach a lesson like she normally does. She was really hush-hush about this. Well, I'm truly her daughter and I'm every bit as direct as she is so of course I asked, "Who was that?"

She knows I'm onto her and she may as well fess up to these shenanigans.

"That was Annie's son. She is having hard times lately so I helped her with her power bill. I told her she didn't have to pay me back but she insisted. I gave her son a few dollars since he dropped it by. He's such a good kid."

"Hold up, wait a minute! He gets $20 dollars for just 'dropping' off money that his mother owes you?"

Of course, I don't ask her this but you better believe I'm thinking this. I don't get $20 for just being nice to her.

What she does next with the money further rattles me. She puts the money in the top kitchen cabinet that we NEVER use. Then she turns and tells me, "There is ALWAYS money somewhere."

A few months go by and strangely enough, it's Annie's son again knocking at the door. I answer the door this time, but he doesn't give me the envelope he's holding in his hand. He says hello, but specifically asks if Ms. Diane is home. I could tell in his face that he was not leaving that envelope with me. He KNEW he wasn't getting $20 from me. She comes to the door and they do their little routine again. He sails off with $20 and she puts the money in the envelope in the top cabinet in the kitchen, again.

It was some years later, I was visiting her and someone knocked at the back door. No, it wasn't Annie's son but it is a similar drill. This time I see her go to the top cabinet in the kitchen to get money and give it to the person at the door. She gave him a separate $20 bill for coming by to pick up the money for his mother. I came to discover that this was her personal "giving fund." Some people would pay her back and others couldn't. Whatever was in there, she would use it to help the next person. If someone paid her back, she would hold it in the top cabinet in the kitchen until someone else had a need. Sometimes, she would be the one with the need, going into the cabinet but most times she would be giving from this money that she had set aside to help others. The stories after her death of how she helped people pay utility bills, buy books for college, and just make ends meet still go on today.

LESSONS FROM MY MOM

10/10/10 – Pay your tithes/Give 10%, Save 10%, and Spend 10% on you.

Treat people well and be generous. God will give you more.

She hated the thought of being labeled as financially illiterate. She felt not having enough had nothing to do with financial literacy.

Single mothers know better than anyone how to make money go as far as it can go and then some. For her, it was a matter of black women and women of color being the lowest paid of all workers.

HOW IT INFUSES THE WORK WE DO TODAY

The grand prize at every event we host in the nonprofit is $300 utility bill payment or rent/mortgage payment. This was inspired by her "kitchen cabinet fund" to help people. Most of the people coming forward with stories of how she helped were either single moms or children of single moms. We also teach financial management in our workshops and coaching program. We continue her legacy of generosity.

THINGS YOU CAN DO RIGHT NOW TO MAKE A DIFFERENCE BY CREATING FINANCIAL WELL-BEING

- 💜 Pay a utility bill for someone. The extra may be needed to buy groceries or medicine or just to make it to another payday.

- 💜 Invest in, promote or buy from small and women owned businesses and nonprofits in your community. Instead of shopping on Black Friday at big establishments, shop small businesses on Small Business Saturday.

- 💜 Give a gift card for a full tank of gas.

- 💜 Buy or prepare dinner for a family to include entrée, sides, dessert and beverage. What a treat!

- 💜 Instead of giving toys, clothes, etc. for birthday gifts, give stocks or mutual funds.

LEAD WITH YOUR HEART
CAREER DEVELOPMENT

It was very early in my career. Against my mother's judgement and ferocious counsel, I pursued Human Resources. All of the stories she would come home and share with me about what not to do as an employee, because of situations she'd experienced in her work in HR, made me more interested in the profession than she could have ever imagined. I followed in her footsteps and left management to pursue a position as an HR Recruiter. She didn't agree at all with my career decision, but like always, she supported me nonetheless.

A few years in, I found myself back in management, but this time, in Human Resources. I loved the work, the people, and the company. However, I had a very demanding boss. While the position and the work challenged me to grow my knowledge and skills, my boss challenged my thinking and core beliefs in a way that made me feel that I had to change myself to fit what the company deemed as right or successful. During a performance appraisal, I received feedback that I needed to make decisions more with my head, not with my heart; which was my tendency. Although the performance review was overall very positive, feedback was often given in the sandwich format, i.e., something good first, the ugly in the middle, and then ending with something good. This bothered me to no end.

The weekend following the performance review, I was visiting my mother. She knew something had me down and didn't gently try to figure it out. She was a "shoot-it-straight" type of person.

"What's bothering you?" she asks.

I tell her about the feedback and she immediately asks me how that made me feel "in my heart." I thought that was so bizarre. I told her I didn't think I could be a successful manager at this company because I always thought about the impact to the people first. It's just how I'm wired.

Her response was, "That's why people will follow you."

She then tells me her story of her career by leading with her heart. She shares that her "claim to fame" was not that she knew all of the HR laws or that she was a whiz at spreadsheets and analyzing data.

She said "I'm good with people. I connect with people, I help people, I correct people, I understand people."

It takes all perspectives, heart and head to run a business. It's inhuman to be in Human Resources and not have a heart for the people. Lead with your heart.

LESSON

After my mom's passing, I received cards, notes, and tributes to her from people who worked with her over the years. Many talked about her heart and how she was fair but firm, how she was honest and straight-forward and how she would tell you the truth but let you keep your dignity.

It was truly a blessing to have my own personal career coach in the same career field to guide me along my career path. We didn't agree necessarily on the career I chose or the decisions I made to leave jobs, but she honored my decisions by always supporting me.

The biggest lesson I learned was to be true to myself and to not be afraid or ashamed to stand in who I am.

HOW IT INFUSES THE WORK WE DO TODAY

In Diane's Heart, we embrace Career Development as one of our pillars. We know that economic well-being and quality of life depends on having adequate income for our moms to take care of themselves and their children. According to The Women's Fund, half of all single moms in Alabama live in poverty. It's the third highest rate in the whole country. Not only do women face barriers including the lack of living wage employment and affordable childcare but their households are at significant risk of experiencing depression, children with behavioral and emotional issues, teen pregnancies or becoming victims of abuse. Our mission at Diane's Heart is to help single moms in Birmingham and surrounding areas rise above these statistics.

THINGS YOU CAN DO RIGHT NOW TO MAKE A DIFFERENCE IN SOMEONE'S CAREER

- ♥ Become a mentor, especially to a black or brown professional in a predominantly white business sector or corporate environment. There are unwritten rules and unspoken requirements that put black and brown professionals in cultural hell when navigating the corporate world. How can you help? By offering to meet every now and then over coffee to answer their questions or share career advice.

- ♥ Volunteer to make a presentation or provide training in your field of business expertise. You may hold a position that someone considers their "dream job."

- ♥ If in a position of authority, promote virtual training and learning.

- Schedule meetings after 10am and before 3pm to allow for flexibility. This could help drop the stress level and allow for more work-life occurrences to happen and not cause additional frustration.

- Help someone write their resume or mock interview. If you've been successful getting a job with your resume or going through an interview, pass along what you did, how you prepared, and what you learned.

THE STORY THAT ALMOST DIDN'T HAPPEN

The nonprofit almost didn't happen. With all of the revelation I received through prayer, meditation and studying the Bible, I was in full disobedience. I was in total fear of the enormity of this mission. Who was I to think that God was really speaking to me? The more I got revelation of what this vision would be, the more afraid I would get. Doubt would flood my mind. Afterall, I had no experience in the nonprofit sector. The most I knew about a nonprofit was volunteering and making a donation. That's all. I stuck the journal I used to record the beautiful journey I was on in a side drawer for almost two years.

It wasn't until I received a call from a dear friend Katrina Wilkins asking, "Whatever happened to the idea of starting a nonprofit?" I had only shared the idea with a few close friends and relatives. I had even reached out to someone I thought surely could help me, but I didn't even receive a call back. However, not Katrina. She would not let it rest. She was all over the internet researching information about starting a nonprofit and discovered it was only $25 to register the organization with the State Treasurer's Office. Although she didn't give the ultimatum, I sensed one was coming. Either I register Diane's Heart with the state or Katrina surely would. So, I did it!

Of the few people I had shared this vision with, there were three who over the years always committed and wanted to help bring it into fruition. Katrina, of course. Stacy Kilcoyne, one of my mother's closest friends that she adored and felt they were kindred spirits. Jermaine Spann, my mother's nephew whom she thought so highly of. This became our Founding Board. A year later, my dear friend and former colleague of over 20 years, Sharon Sherrod and Mary Walton, a dear friend of over 30 years from high school and college joined in with us. Most recently, Yelonda Jones, a friend and former colleague of over 15 years is helping us to continue to build and grow. In the background is my dear friend C. René Washington who has encouraged and coached me and supported the nonprofit the whole way.

It is with this team of people, who like my mom have loving hearts and generous spirits, along with my aunts Gloria Gossom, Cynthia Martin, my uncle Kenneth Hill and countless numbers of family members, volunteers, donors, participants and sponsors who have helped me build Diane's Heart in service to single mothers and their children. I'm forever grateful.

> *"Continue. And by doing so*
> *You and your work*
> *Will be able to continue*
> *Eternally."*
>
> BY MAYA ANGELOU

DIANE'S HEART IS MY HEART

We are taught how to love. My mother modeled how to love in the most beautiful way. Her way of loving was very pure and Christ-like. Thank you for going with me through the memories and lessons my mother taught me by example and by faith. I pray something that I've shared sparks inspiration in your heart to make a difference in your corner of the world. If in tragedy or loss, I pray this fuels you to overcome evil with good. You are the answer to someone's problem. Your heart contains your gift. If fear has a grip on you, my prayer is that you go from running from purpose to chasing it.

ABOUT THE AUTHOR

Tonya Hill Allen is the Founder and Executive Director of Diane's Heart. Diane's Heart is her passion and Life's work. As a Certified Executive Coach, she is also CEO of Falala Life where she uses her coaching and consulting expertise to help clients create the life, career or business they love. She has over 25 years in Human Resources and Talent Management leadership expertise of which she uses to guide clients to tap into their light and live in purpose.

www.ingramcontent.com/pod-product-compliance
Lightning Source LLC
Chambersburg PA
CBHW021431070526
44577CB00001B/164